D1544482

POLICE
ROBOTS

BY ELIZABETH NOLL

Blastoff! Discovery launches
a new mission: reading to learn.
Filled with facts and features,
each book offers you an exciting
new world to explore!

This edition first published in 2018 by Bellwether Media, Inc.

No part of this publication may be reproduced in whole or in
part without written permission of the publisher.
For information regarding permission, write to Bellwether
Media, Inc., Attention: Permissions Department,
5357 Penn Avenue South, Minneapolis, MN 55419.

Library of Congress Cataloging-in-Publication Data

Names: Noll, Elizabeth, author.
Title: Police Robots / by Elizabeth Noll.
Description: Minneapolis, MN : Bellwether Media, Inc., [2018]
    | Series: Blastoff! Discovery: World of Robots | Audience:
    Age: 7-13. | Includes bibliographical references and index.
Identifiers: LCCN 2016059017 (print) | LCCN 2017021721
    (ebook) | ISBN 9781626176911 (hardcover : alk. paper)
    | ISBN 9781681034218 (ebook)
    | ISBN 9781618912947 (paperback : alk. paper)
Subjects: LCSH: Police–Equipment and supplies–Juvenile
    literature. | Robots–Juvenile literature.
Classification: LCC HV7936.E7 (ebook) | LCC HV7936.E7
    N645 2018 (print) | DDC 363.2028/4–dc23
LC record available at https://lccn.loc.gov/2016059017

Editor: Christina Leaf   Designer: Jon Eppard

Printed in the United States of America, North Mankato, MN.

TABLE OF CONTENTS

POLICE ROBOT AT WORK!

Crowds were already filling the street for the big event. But Officer Erwin had work to do. He was on the bomb squad, and they needed to search for explosives in the crowd.

He set up a robot to explore the streets. Other officers told the crowds to move back as the robot moved about. Officer Erwin directed the robot near a trash can. There, the robot's **sensors** picked up a dangerous mix of chemicals.

Remotec F5A

The robot reached into the trash can with its long arm. The claw at the end of the arm carefully grabbed a small package. It was a bomb!

Slowly, the robot removed the bomb from the trash can. Officer Erwin then directed it toward an open area away from any buildings or crowds. There, the robot safely disabled the bomb. Thanks to the robot, the bomb did not harm anyone!

WHAT ARE POLICE ROBOTS?

Police robots are often used in dangerous situations. They can take the place of human officers. Bomb **disposal** robots are the most common. Other robots help police figure out where criminals are hiding.

Robots also help in less dangerous situations. They can direct traffic at crowded **intersections**. Some work in search and rescue. They can move through spaces too small for an officer. Some can crash through barriers to find criminals.

WHEN ROBOTS FLY

Some police departments have unmanned aerial vehicles (UAVs), also called drones.

Police robots come in many shapes and sizes. The smallest weigh about 1 pound (0.4 kilograms) and could fit in a shoebox. The largest weigh almost 20 tons (18,144 kilograms).

Many police robots are designed to gather information with cameras and **two-way radios**. These take videos and record and **broadcast** sound. Then the robots can go into buildings where armed suspects are hiding.

tEODor UGV

treads

Most police robots can move using wheels or treads. They are called unmanned ground vehicles (UGVs). Some UGVs are controlled remotely. A human operator stays in a safe place. Other robots use sensors and computer programs to **navigate** on their own.

These robots might get shot or blown up. However, this is better than a human police officer getting injured or killed.

THE DEVELOPMENT OF POLICE ROBOTS

Early police robots were mainly used for bomb disposal. The idea probably came from a 1972 invention used by the British Army. The Wheelbarrow was an electronic wheelbarrow used to disable bombs.

In the early 2000s, the United States military began to give their old robots to police departments. The most common ex-military robots used on police forces are UGVs like PackBot and MARCbot IV. In the military, these are called **explosive ordnance disposal** (EOD) robots.

Wheelbarrow

HAND-ME-DOWNS

The U.S. military has given nearly 1,000 robots to U.S. police.

MARCbot IV

PackBot

Surplus military robots are now in hundreds of police departments across the country. Some people believe this is a problem. They worry that police robots could be used to harm innocent people. Others fear a loss of privacy. Computer experts also say robots could be **hacked**.

Other people say police robots are an important addition to police forces. They have already saved the lives of officers and citizens. Police in big cities may deal with bomb scares every day. Thanks to robots, their risk is much smaller.

As U.S. wars have wound down, the number of extra military robots has risen. As a result, police robots have become much more common.

At the same time, hardware and sensors have become smaller and faster. This has led to robots that are cheaper and more powerful. Some police departments can now afford to buy their own robots.

Lawmakers are working on policies that control the way police use robots. They hope to make sure police robots are not misused.

POLICE ROBOT PROFILE:
BATCAT

Imagine a gigantic forklift with a **telescoping** claw that can lift cars and crush houses. That's BatCat.

The Los Angeles Police Department was looking for new ways to protect its officers. It asked for a heavy-duty machine that could move without a driver. **Autonomous** Solutions used a Caterpillar **telehandler** base to create this extremely large, powerful robot. With accessories, it cost nearly $1 million.

BatCat has cameras and sensors that allow it to be controlled remotely. Officers stay safe while BatCat handles bombs or **breaches** buildings where armed criminals are hiding.

HEAVY LIFTER

BatCat can lift 12,000 pounds (5,443 kilograms). This means it can pick up a car bomb and move it to a safe location.

Name:	Bomb Assessment Tactical Counter Assault Tool
Nickname:	BatCat
Developer:	Autonomous Solutions (ASI) with Northop Grumman Remotec
Release Date:	2009
Functions:	bomb disposal, barricade breaching
Size:	39,000 pounds (17,690 kilograms); about 8 feet (2.4 meters) high; about 20 feet (6.1 meters) long
Speed:	6 miles (9.7 kilometers) per hour
Reach:	50 feet (15.2 meters), horizontal and vertical

POLICE ROBOT PROFILE:
REMOTEC ANDROS F6A

The Remotec Andros F6A is one of the most popular robots on police forces. This UGV is often used to find and disable bombs. A human operator watches on a screen as the robot sends back images with its many cameras. Some cameras can even function in the dark!

The F6A can be used for more than just finding bombs. Police officers can add tools for different jobs. One is used to break windows. Another can cut heavy cables. The F6A can even have a circular saw attached!

Name:	Remotec Andros F6A
Developer:	Northrup Grumman
Release Date:	2011
Functions:	patrolling, gathering information, bomb disposal
Size:	4.3 feet (1.3 meters) long; 2.4 feet (0.7 meters) wide; 4.7 feet (1.4 meters) high
Speed:	3.5 miles (5.6 kilometers) per hour
Reach:	4.7 feet (1.4 meters) horizontal; 9 feet (2.7 meters) vertical

POLICE ROBOT PROFILE: DRC TRAFFIC ROBOT

In the Democratic Republic of the Congo (DRC), traffic was a big problem. People did not respect traffic officers and broke laws often. Thérèse Izay Kirongozi came up with a creative solution. She had the idea to use traffic robots.

Today, five giant **humanoid** robots help control traffic in Kinshasa, DRC. The rotating, **solar-powered** robots have red and green lights on their arms and chests. The lights tell walkers and drivers when to stop and when to go. If someone breaks a law, video cameras in the robot's eyes record it.

IN STYLE

Since local police often wear sunglasses, the designer gave the robots sunglasses.

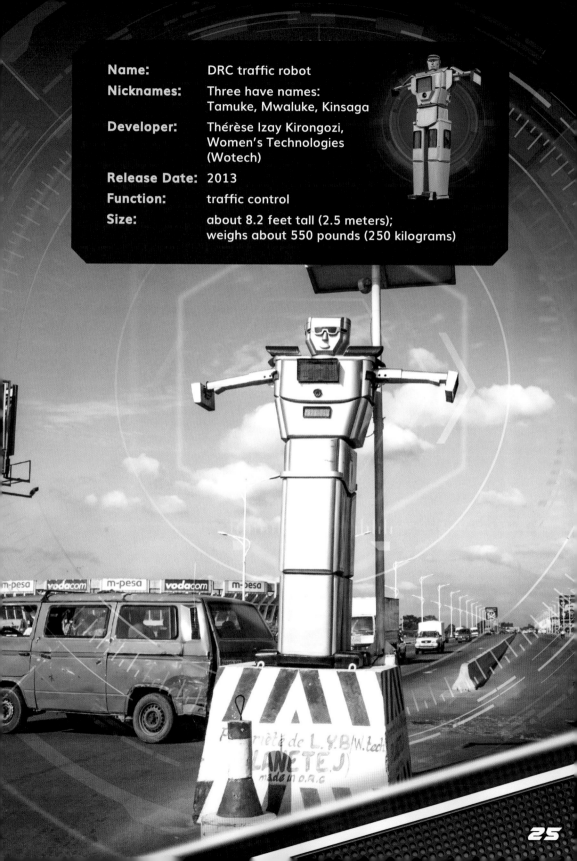

Name:	DRC traffic robot
Nicknames:	Three have names: Tamuke, Mwaluke, Kinsaga
Developer:	Thérèse Izay Kirongozi, Women's Technologies (Wotech)
Release Date:	2013
Function:	traffic control
Size:	about 8.2 feet tall (2.5 meters); weighs about 550 pounds (250 kilograms)

POLICE ROBOT PROFILE:

K5

K5 looks a little like it belongs in Star Wars. This autonomous robotic security guard patrols places such as shopping malls and parking lots. It takes in information with cameras, a microphone, sensors including **LIDAR** and **GPS**, and other tools. It can scan and remember license plates.

K5 does not try to stop crimes. The information K5 gathers goes to humans, who decide what to do. What about crimes to K5 itself? The robot's 300-pound (136-kilogram) body makes it hard to knock over!

HIGH TECH

K5 moves around using technology similar to driverless cars.

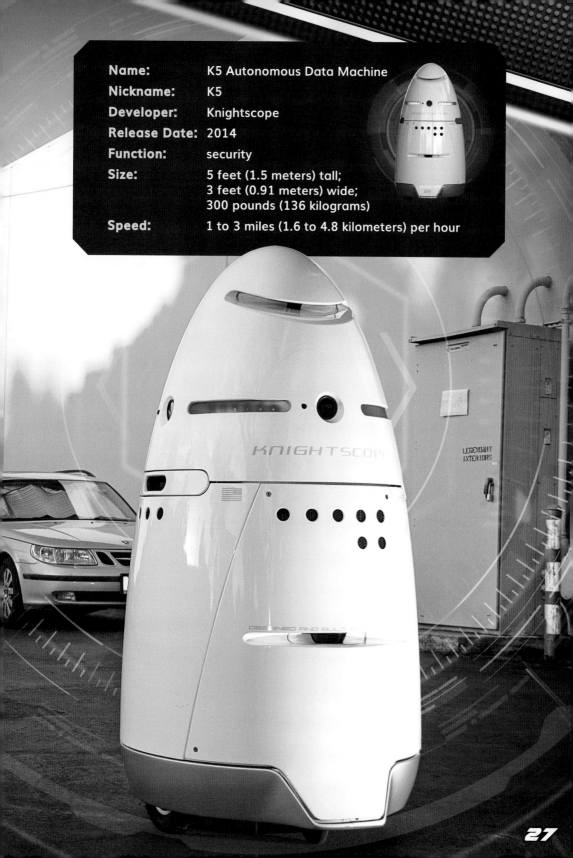

Name:	K5 Autonomous Data Machine
Nickname:	K5
Developer:	Knightscope
Release Date:	2014
Function:	security
Size:	5 feet (1.5 meters) tall; 3 feet (0.91 meters) wide; 300 pounds (136 kilograms)
Speed:	1 to 3 miles (1.6 to 4.8 kilometers) per hour

THE FUTURE OF POLICE ROBOTS

As robotic technology improves, police robots will become more advanced. They will become more common, too, as long as the military surplus program continues.

Police robots have already saved the lives of hundreds of officers and citizens. But many people still have concerns about using them. Many experts say we need new laws to cover the use of police robots. By working together, communities can find the best and safest uses for robots on police forces.

GLOSSARY

autonomous—able to act without help

breaches—breaks through or makes an opening in something

broadcast—to put forth sound or images

disposal—the act of getting rid of something

explosive ordnance disposal—the act of getting rid of bombs

GPS—short for global positioning system; GPS is a navigational system that uses satellites to determine locations on Earth.

hacked—broken into, in relation to computers and other technology

humanoid—having a human-like shape

intersections—places where two or more roads meet

LIDAR—short for light detection and ranging; LIDAR is a method of measuring distance using a laser.

navigate—to figure out how to get from one place to another

sensors—devices that respond to light, pressure, sound, or other physical changes

solar-powered—powered by the sun

surplus—extra

telehandler—a machine with a telescoping arm that can carry heavy loads

telescoping—able to shrink down by having one part slide into another

two-way radios—radios that can send and receive sound

TO LEARN MORE

AT THE LIBRARY

Faust, Daniel R. *Military and Police Robots*. New York, N.Y.: PowerKids Press, 2016.

Noll, Elizabeth. *Military Robots*. Minneapolis, Minn.: Bellwether Media, 2018.

Spilsbury, Richard and Louise. *Robots in Law Enforcement*. New York, N.Y.: Gareth Stevens Publishing, 2016.

ON THE WEB

Learning more about police robots is as easy as 1, 2, 3.

1. Go to www.factsurfer.com.

2. Enter "police robots" into the search box.

3. Click the "Surf" button and you will see a list of related web sites.

With factsurfer.com, finding more information is just a click away.

INDEX